RISE *and* FALL

John Dickson
Laurie Walker

AGNES ETHERINGTON ART CENTRE, KINGSTON

MACDONALD STEWART ART CENTRE, GUELPH

PLUG IN INC., WINNIPEG

1996

CONTENTS

———◆———

FOREWORD

———◆———

This collaborative publication brings together the work of two artists and three curators. The convergence of curatorial interest on the work of Canadian artists Laurie Walker and John Dickson attests to the compelling rigour of their art and the fact that in many ways it eloquently captures the tenor of the times. In-tandem consideration of the work of these two artists allows assessment of their work and by inference, of the concerns of an emerging generation of artists. Jan Allen discusses the theoretical intersection of the two bodies of work and the relevance of the motif of cyclicity to this cultural moment. Nancy Campbell examines change as both metaphor and methodology in Laurie Walker's recent work, while Wayne Baerwaldt's essay focuses on the recoding of spectacle in John Dickson's art as it is achieved through an arch blend of performative movement and active indifference.

Three exhibitions are documented and interpreted in this publication: *John Dickson* at Plug In Inc. and John Dickson and Laurie Walker in related versions of *Rise and Fall* at the Agnes Etherington and Macdonald Stewart Art Centres. We acknowledge with gratitude the gracious participation of the artists, the contributions of staff at the three galleries, and the spirit of co-operation that animated the curatorial collaboration.

Jan Allen, Agnes Etherington Art Centre
Wayne Baerwaldt, Plug In Inc.
Nancy Campbell, Macdonald Stewart Art Centre

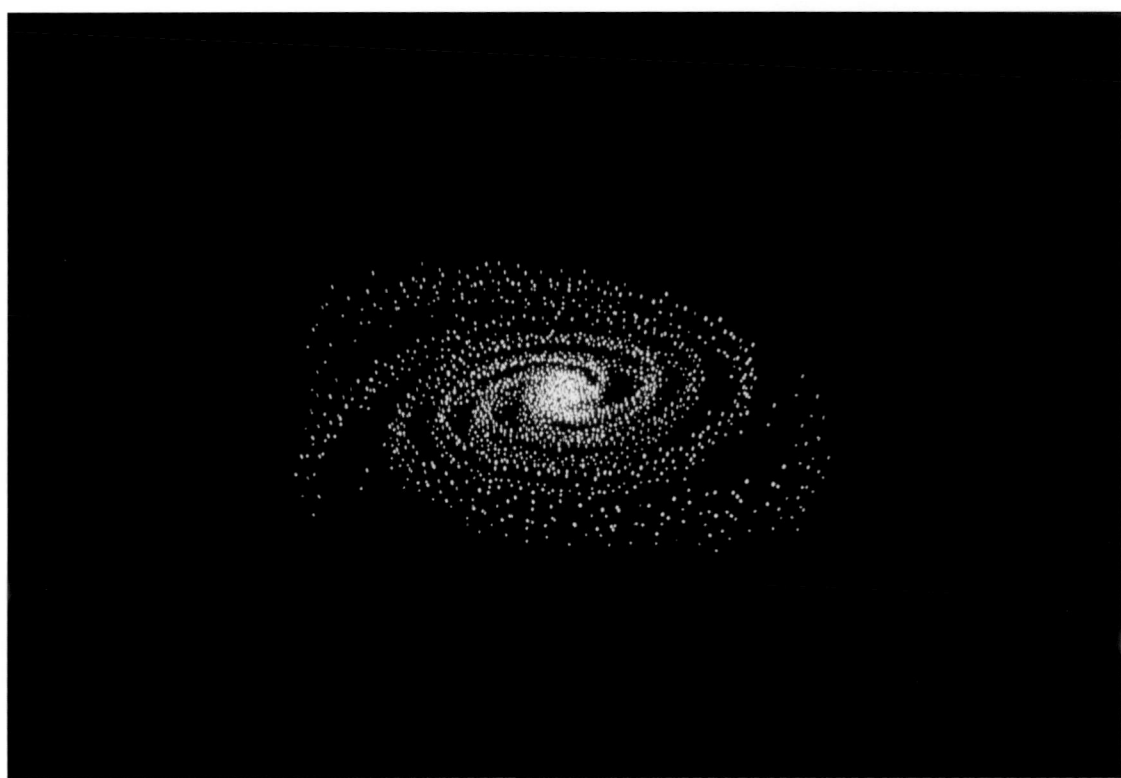

John Dickson, *Vertigo* (1995) (Detail)

Spin Cycle

Jan Allen

. . . where everything so rapidly assumed the appearance of a rise, a fall.[1]

Writing in the late 1920s, Surrealist poet André Breton thus described the state of extreme perceptual vulnerability of the madwoman Nadja. In Breton's view, madness was the price Nadja paid for too great an awareness of the perpetual, rhythmic instability beneath tangible reality.

I PAUSE TO THINK, MY FINGER RESTING ABSENT-MINDEDLY ON THE PAGE-DOWN KEY OF MY LAP-TOP. A FLURRIED SENSATION OF FALLING BRINGS ME TO A SOFT LANDING ON A BLANK PAGE 14. I CLAMBER BACK UP TO THE LOWER FRINGE OF THE TEXT, WHERE I CLING, HOPING FOR SURER FOOTING.

The place to start, of course, is not with Breton's vertiginous text, but with the two exceptional young artists and their work and why they might be considered together here. John Dickson and Laurie Walker work separately, in Toronto and Montreal respectively, virtually unaware of one another's work. While the dyad of the two-person show risks aesthetic gridlock in the absence of a mediating third, in this case the tension between the two practices is not flat and rigid, but that of a sweet and moving logic.

The exhibition's title, *Rise and Fall* (taken from one of John Dickson's pieces) refers to the rhythmic movement that is an overriding element in the work of both artists. Dickson and Walker evoke the standing cycles of nature and culture, of flesh and spirit, expressing these processes in forms and installation pieces. There is an element of animism at work here: the mimesis of biological and cosmic process elides the boundaries between living and non-living matter in an unsettling and pleasurable confusion of categories. One thinks, again, of the Surrealists and the delight they took in mechanomorphic invention.

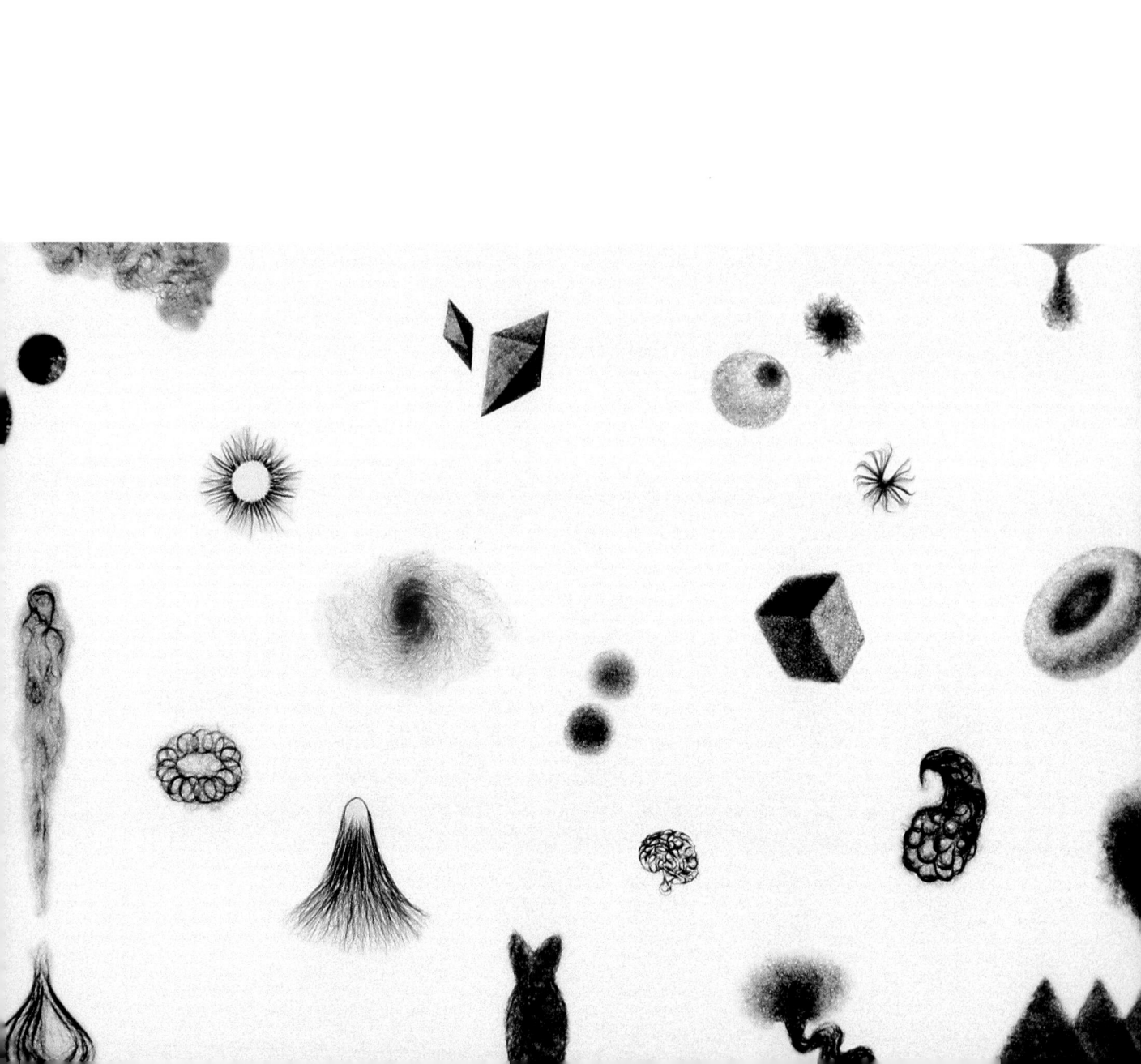

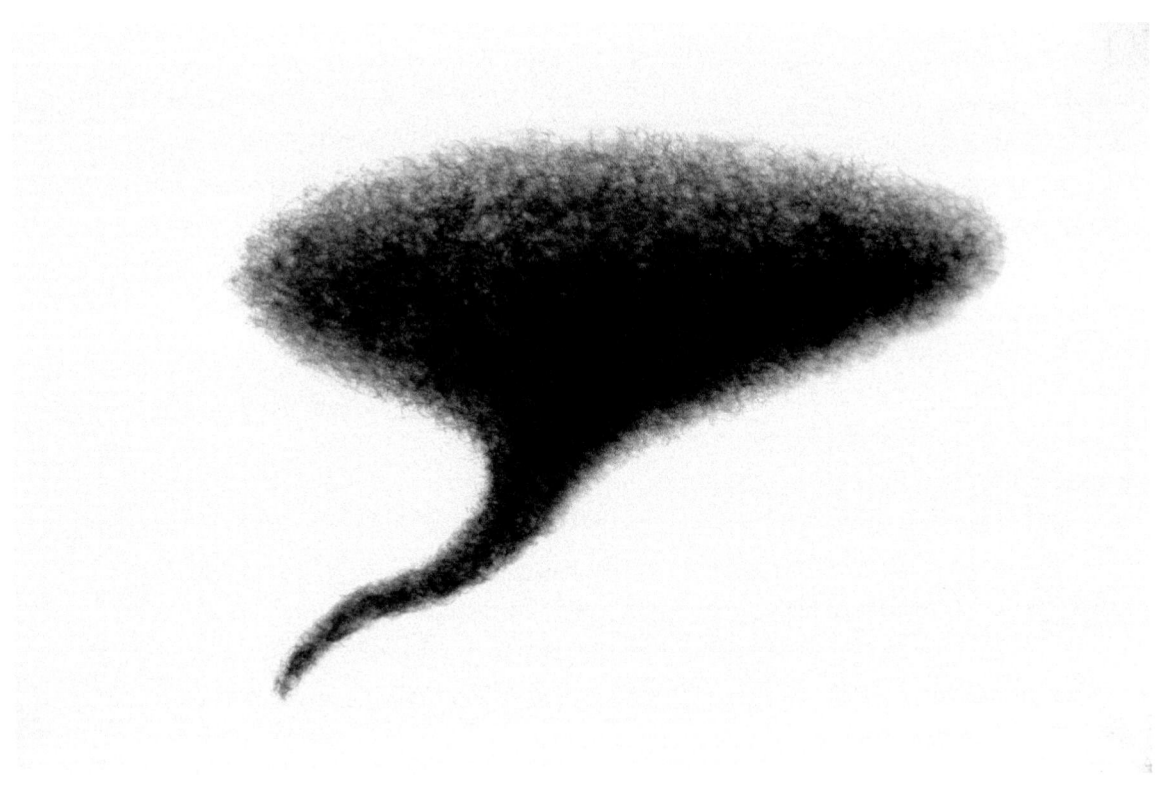

Opposite: John Dickson, *Hair Drawings* (1990–94)
Above: John Dickson, *Tornado* (1994)

The similarities here, in terms of cyclicity and biological references, throw into relief the subtle metaphysical differences in the two artists' work. Through allusion to great cultural traditions and belief systems, Laurie Walker's sculpture speaks of the possibility of transcendence or redemption: wisdom is available and methods for attaining a measure of harmony between self and the world have been mapped out by those before us. In contrast, the secularity of John Dickson's work presents a resilient materialism in which grace lies in steadfast observation of its own persistent cycles. In both cases, a rhythmic pulse is posited as the matrix in which all experience is embedded, a kind of existential binary code. Although it may be tempting to read the differences in Dickson's and Walker's works in terms of determinant stereotypes of gender or region, their stances are better understood as two coexisting streams within culture. We have reached a point where neither faith nor its denial is ultimately sustainable.

The conceptual content of Dickson's and Walker's art is leavened by hyperbole. The works set up a deft oscillation between profundity and outlandishness, an instability of voice that mates happily with the restless circulation of fluids and references within the pieces. Consider the eye pieces. John Dickson's *Crying Eye* and Laurie Walker's *Seeing Blue* participate in the proliferation of the eye motif in contemporary art, evident in diverse works, from Michael Snow's *Conception of Light* (1992) through Tran T. Kim-Trang's series of videotapes on blindness (1993–). In *Crying Eye*, a life-size plastic eyeball nestled in the surface of the wall weeps quietly. In *Seeing Blue*, the motion is reversed: an enormous, carved-sponge brain soaks up metaphorical comprehension from fluid-filled, eggshell eyeballs, passive receptacles thrust heavenward for inspiration.

I CATCH MYSELF LEANING BACK, THIS TIME MOVING MY ORBS INTO POSITION TO THINK ABOUT THOSE EGGSHELLS IN A REFLEXIVE INVOCATION OF ALCHEMICAL SYMPATHY.

There is a breath-taking literalism in both these pieces that speaks to the viewer's awareness of his or her own body. If the extrication of biological parts from supporting systems — also evident in *Rise and Fall* and *Ashen Wing* — is discomfiting, the enactment of bodily processes compels identification.

Seeing Blue models a biological system and refers to the explanatory schema for life processes set forth by science, myth, and religion. Seeing and the mechanics of vision are presented as metaphors for the intellectual and spiritual quest to comprehend the world. In Laurie Walker's unpublished proposal for the piece (1993), she quotes Ralph Waldo Emerson's "The Poet" (1844):

Opposite: Laurie Walker, *Seeing Blue* (1993–94)

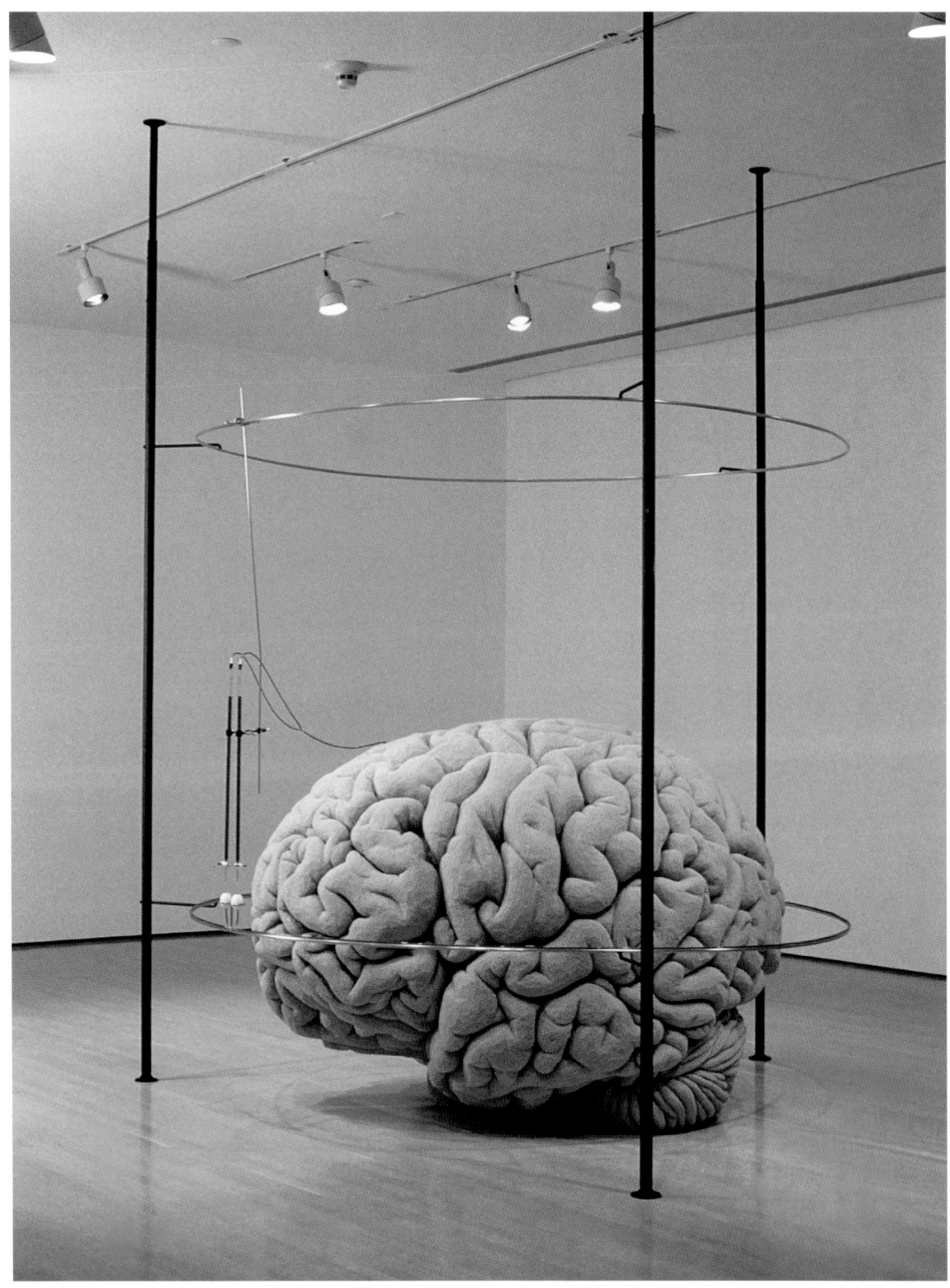

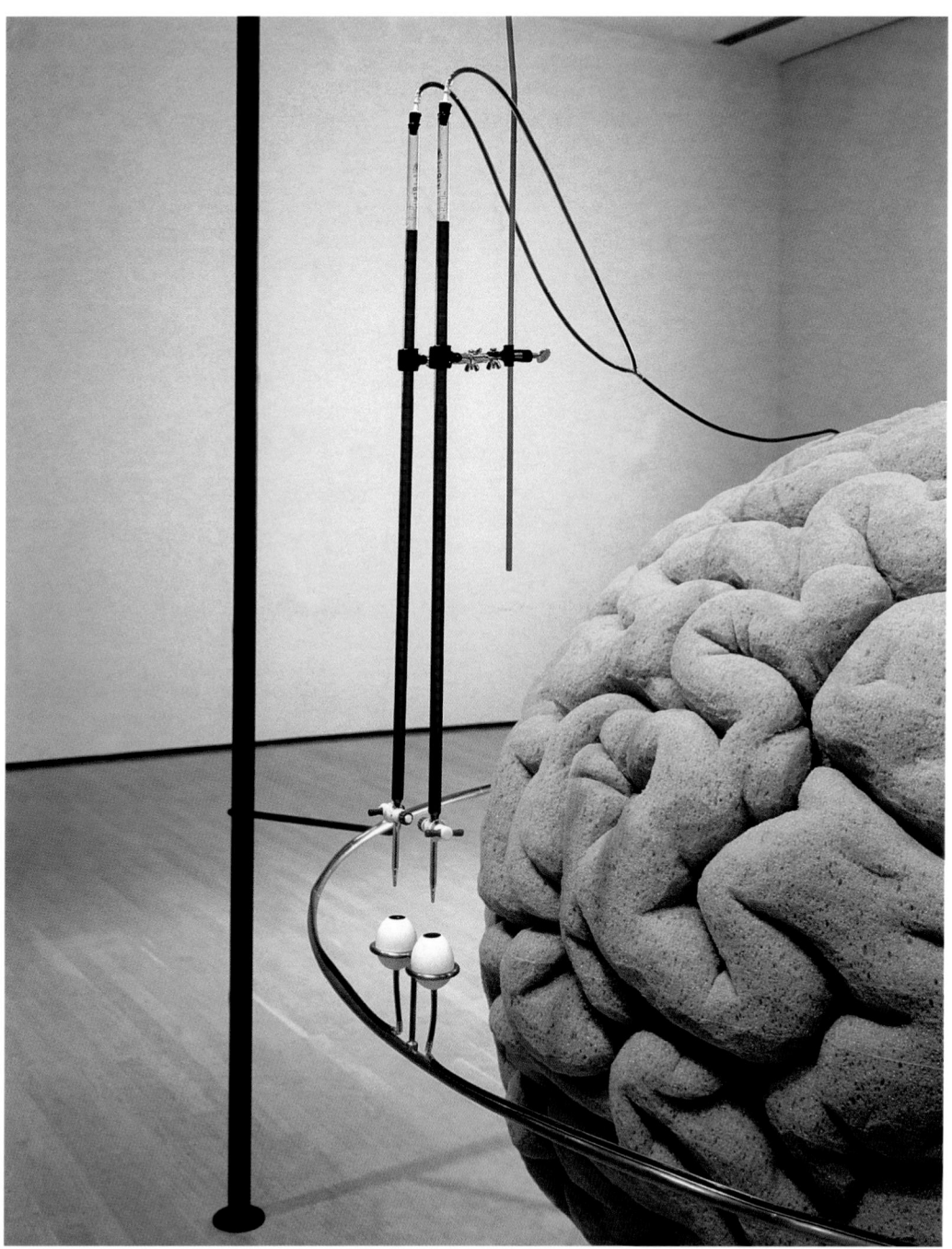

Above: *Seeing Blue* (Detail)

> This insight, which expresses itself by what is called Imagination, is a very high sort of seeing, which does not come by study, but by the intellect being where and what it sees, by sharing the path or circuit of things through forms, and so making them translucid to others.[2]

The hoops and burettes of *Seeing Blue* set up an implicit movement of fluid in its passage from blue to green, thus marking out the alchemy of consciousness in a bio-circuit that discerns the cycles of existence.

The six meticulously rendered watercolour images of *Seeing Blue* act as predella to the "altarpiece" of the big brain. The filigreed cross-section of the brain, the alchemical flowers, the ouroboros, and the vinegar-filled sponge proffered to the crucified Christ ("I thirst") all speak of the craving for knowledge that drives our species. We trace patterns and speculate on hidden relationships between disparate forms.

John Dickson describes *Crying Eye* as "an emotional trigger," the meaning of which is shaped by context. A response to the misery the artist witnessed on the streets of San Francisco, the piece was initially exhibited in the seedy confines of a room in the Duke of Connaught Hotel in Toronto.[3] Its presentation in the Agnes Etherington's Main Gallery brings out the B-movie excess of *Crying Eye* while connecting it through proximity to its art historical precedents.[4]

In Jacques Derrida's *Memoirs of the Blind*, blindness is reckoned as the human condition. The unseeing eye fixed open is a motif of a forced witness unable to penetrate the multiple and shifting forms of reality. The price of consciousness lies in painful awareness of the profound limits of both comprehension and compassion. Derrida ends his text by linking vision and emotion, which he posits as quintessentially human traits. He cites a passage from poet Andrew Marvell that echoes the synthesis of sight and sorrow found in *Crying Eye*:

> Thus let your streams o'erflow your springs,
> Till eyes and tears be the same things:
> And each the other's difference bears;
> These weeping eyes, those seeing tears.[5]

The mute grief of the wall in *Crying Eye* is implicitly cyclical insofar as there is constant seepage and replenishment. Here, tears slip unabashedly down the wall in a slow trickle that conjures irrational empathy in the viewer. The subtlety of the movement is compelling: the mimesis of responsiveness prompts the viewer to wait for each tear like a believer before a miraculous breach of the possible.

Walker's *Ashen Wing* and Dickson's *Rise and Fall* refer to the rhythmic alternation of the forces of destruction and restoration, expulsion and replenishment. In both cases a biological fragment is the node of cyclical enactment. The juxtaposition of Walker's organo-mythological work with Dickson's bio-industrial form suggests the existence of a pervasive cosmic rhythm of energy.

In *Rise and Fall*, the cycle plays out in the surge and drainage of bodily fluid. The body is rendered as an oversized hand and gonadal sack animated by a lethargic pulse along their conjoining tube. *Rise and Fall* reads as a bathetic schema of human effort reduced to base physical function, incessantly doing and procreating (or at least copulating). Suspended in the gallery, water moves beneath the dense industrial skin of rubberized canvas like a passive sigh.

Ashen Wing is an ash-covered goose wing with mirrored underside installed on the gallery wall in flight position. It is an emblem of the phoenix, the mythical Arabian bird that stands for all things restored after apparent annihilation. Walker's piece collapses the narrative of the phoenix, condensing it into a single point: from the wing dredged in ashes, burning is implicit in flight. What is more, *Ashen Wing* is engaged in an impossible effort: it will never lift that wall but it is always rising and falling. The work suggests that no steady state is possible but that an equilibrium emerges across the span of time. We live in a flux of movement, perpetually overcoming difficulty. The mirrored fragments on the underwing are poised, like some tiny, inverted bank of solar panels, to catch an updraft of hope.

The most recent works for both artists coalesce the rise and fall to a steady whirl. Laurie Walker's *Prayer Beads* is an oversized rosary, a string of stones encased in pigs' bladders. The taut, crackled surfaces of the stones conjure up the frailty of the flesh. Each stone is drilled and strung on a plastic tube filled with red wine; the resulting startling device is at once suggestive of the eucharist, bodily systems, and medicine. Walker's use of such ordinary materials as stones and plastic tubing lends a sense of pragmatic function to this form for restoring the relationship between the faithful and cosmic order. *Prayer Beads* is inscribed with Buddhist, Christian, Muslim and Hindu prayers. The artist's interest here is in the pervasive human ritual of cyclical counted prayer. Belief in the capacity of an object to function as a vehicle of intention or spirit is fundamental to this practice. When ritual praise or calls for intercession invoke the divine through material engagement of body and objects, faith provides its own logic in a surge of movement that overrides circumstance.

I RECALL LEAVING LAURIE'S STUDIO LAST YEAR, STILL THINKING ABOUT THIS WORK. I BOARDED THE BUS DOWN AVENUE DU PARC AND, AS I SETTLED INTO MY SEAT, I NOTICED THAT THE WOMAN ACROSS FROM ME WAS FINGERING A ROSARY, HER LIPS MOVING IN SILENT PRAYER. AT THAT MOMENT, I SENSED THE REPLICATION OF THIS SMALL RITE OF SOLACE IN THE HEARTS AND HANDS OF MILLIONS AROUND THE GLOBE.

John Dickson's most recent work *Vertigo* is an environment — whether installed in the gloriously crumbling, abandoned industrial site where it was first exhibited, or in the dark hush of the art gallery.[6] The twinkle of spiralling lights, the steady rush of the standing whorl of water, and the monotone countdown of the audio tape have a wonderful, mesmerizing effect. *The Globe and Mail* critic John Bentley Mays came close to capturing the piece in his suggestion that it is about entropy: "a reminder of the relentless wind-down of closed systems."[7] But *Vertigo* is not winding down; rather, it layers together sets of cycles that stubbornly sustain their form.

Parallel reductive systems intersect in *Vertigo*. Galactic little lights reflect on glass panels and subsequently (much distorted) on the surface of the whirlpool. The vortex of the sound component is implicit in the direction of counting and in the compression of interval around zero and is explicit in the rotation of the broadcast through six speakers in turn. From one hundred to minus one hundred, the logic closes and expands like a whirlpool, like a galaxy.

THE NUMBERS PACE AROUND THE ROOM IN A SLOW SPIN, MARKING OUT THE PASSAGE OF TIME. JOHN SAYS THAT ZERO IS LIKE THE CENTRE OF A VORTEX; LIKE A BLACK HOLE, IT IS A COMPRESSION THAT IS AN ABSENCE. COUNTING BACKWARDS WAS HIS CHILDHOOD METHOD FOR FALLING ASLEEP; HE RECALLS THE SLIPPAGE THAT DEVELOPED AS THE NUMBERS PASSED ZERO AND HE SANK INTO THE TEMPORARY OBLIVION OF SLEEP.

Dickson's use of water is sensitive to the emotional resonance of the medium, which he explains in terms of its "chaotic untidiness," that is, its refusal of containment and the ever-present hazard of the spills and leaks that signal abjection. By harnessing water within mechanical systems, Dickson amplifies viewer identification with the work. We are, after all, watery beings who recognize ourselves as standing patterns of energy, governed by rhythms and definitive circulating systems. Congruence of physical and symbolic function in these works generates a perfect vacillation between literal and cultural meaning. Dickson's mingling of mechanical systems and water place nature and technology on a continuum, much as Laurie Walker does nature and culture. We are left, not with Nadja's madness, but with wonder in the face of an ordinary world filled with swaying possibilities and veiled intersections.

The motif of cyclicity in the exhibition *Rise and Fall* enacts a give and take of systems that builds across time: cyclicity functions as both a formal and an emblematic denial of fixed position. In rendering cyclicity beautiful the works in *Rise and Fall* offer a structure of continuance to counter the pervasive end anxiety associated with the close of the second millennium. Given the rapid rate of technological and social change in the past century transformation itself has become a constant. In such a context comfort may be found in motion. Ultimately, the cycle's will to continue is reassuring, subverting as it does the possibility of conclusion.

Endnotes

1. André Breton, *Nadja*, trans. R. Howard (New York: Grove Press, 1960), 135.

2. Ralph Waldo Emerson, *The Selected Writings of Ralph Waldo Emerson* (New York: Penguin, 1965), 318.

3. *Duke-u-menta*, Toronto, 1994.

4. Coincidentally, an exquisite sixteenth-century painting of a weeping Christ as the Man of Sorrows hangs in another space at the Art Centre.

5. Andrew Marvell, "Eyes and Tears," cited in Jacques Derrida, *Memoirs d'aveugle: Autoportrait et autres ruines* (Paris: Éditions de la Réunion des musées nationaux, 1990), 130.

6. The piece was first shown in the exhibition *Votive Chamber* by the Nether Mind artists' collective, Toronto, 1995.

7. "Two shows that show the unstoppable," *The Globe and Mail* (Toronto), 9 September 1995, C17.

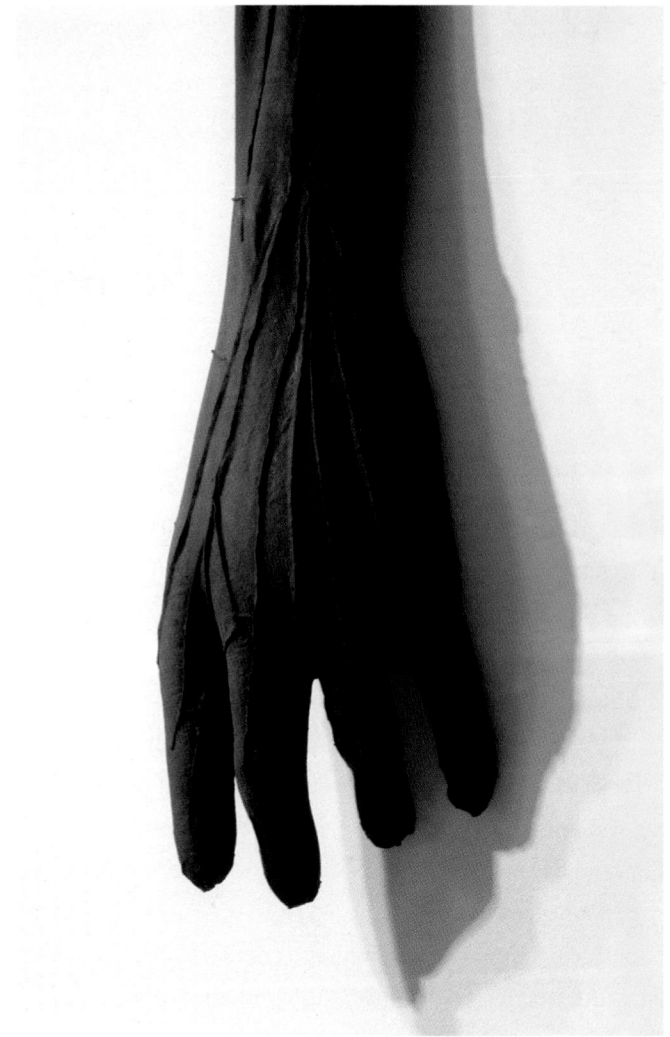

John Dickson, *Rise and Fall* (1993) (Detail)

John Dickson

— Black Rubber, Hair, Water, Prosthetic Devices, Low Lights, No Spectacles

Wayne Baerwaldt

When the "spectacle" in art is engaged, the potential for a break with tradition is anticipated, intimately connected as it is to the eruption of daring, creative energies that can restore a viewer's faith in the vision quests of artists. Commonly defined as an unusual, grand public show or scene, the dimensions of the spectacle can be awesome and overwhelming to the status quo. Flash points in recent art history — such as Happenings, the antics of the Viennese Aktionists, the Situationist International, Destruction in Art summits, and even the posturing of punk rock music — constructed spectacle in opposition to a widely experienced, nullifying alienation from work and life. Art spectacles had flair and purpose and an immoral air about them. During the 1980s, art spectacles became more personable as the media-art star entered the artworld and the tabloids, the predictable effect of a fickle artworld that had grown increasingly dependent on crass self-promotion and the supply and demand reactions of the market. The art spectacle seemed to become bigger and bolder than ever and the marginal artworld indignantly claimed the most perverse statement as a stroke of enlightenment. In the early 1990s, artists even went on to make movies in which the pure form of the silver screen periodically regained its high, spectacular glow.

The spectacle as a key to enlightenment based on a work of art is rare. Spectacle is just as commonly associated with farce and failure as it is with any attempt to produce aesthetic breaks or other changes of substance. Furthermore, consideration of spectacle as an ideological and aesthetic tool cannot be restricted to deserving projects such as the Situationist

International from Guy Debord's *Society of the Spectacle* (1967). The definition of spectacle shifts incessantly; its social and personal applications remain uncertain and its scale indeterminate, a situation exemplified in the following random excerpt from a *New Yorker* article by Louis Begley:

> I was about to skip all the way to world weather when a little Swissair ad in the upper-left-hand corner, in the same place where the New York Times makes its claims about all the news that's fit to print, arrested my attention: it had in it a splash of red as bright as blood. There were two other items in color on the page, but they were subdued.... But only the words printed in the eye-catching red mattered to me: they were "Time is everything."[1]

"Time is everything" is a quaint colloquialism but for this author it attains the status of minor spectacle; as he later admits, he is "shaken by the truth it revealed." Spectacles should accomplish this much. Begley goes on to explore his mundane professional, personal and familial obligations, often overwhelming obligations that are reduced to the scheduled grid of units of time, each one-tenth of an hour, established by the legal profession as units of payment for services rendered. His response to a detail in the *New York Times*, a minute bit of print media, indicates just how subtle and insidious spectacles can be; their complex and coded surfaces can lay open a hidden personal and social dynamic. A genuine spectacle can induce personal revelation to an extent that is inversely proportionate to the spectacle's size, format and apparent content.

The Canadian artist John Dickson is reluctant to apply any sense of the word spectacle to his intimately felt, large-scale, mixed-media sculptures and drawings. Dickson insists that the common definition of spectacle as blockbuster public event is inadequate and misleading as it obscures the more important issues and subtle strategies behind his "minor spectacles."[2] Dickson may be willing to embrace "minor spectacle" as a descriptive term, albeit with multiple clauses and conditions attached. Another relevant term is "active indifference," the quality Georges Bataille detected in the resonant paintings of Monet. Dickson's "active indifference" offers a subtle audaciousness in proposing doses of both eroticism and animal instinct. His concern with seemingly unstable volumes, reductive surfaces, limited colours, sickly humour and mysterious sources (i.e., fecund water) suggests that he does celebrate spectacle, if somewhat reluctantly.

Dickson's sculptures are enigmatically rich, fluid, mixed-media constructions that when properly lit and given room to breathe are exhilarating and uncanny. The rubberized black cotton material of *Strange Fruit* (1993) encloses and maintains two bulbous, huge "drops" of water that gravity cannot command. Three and a half metres of webbed rubber

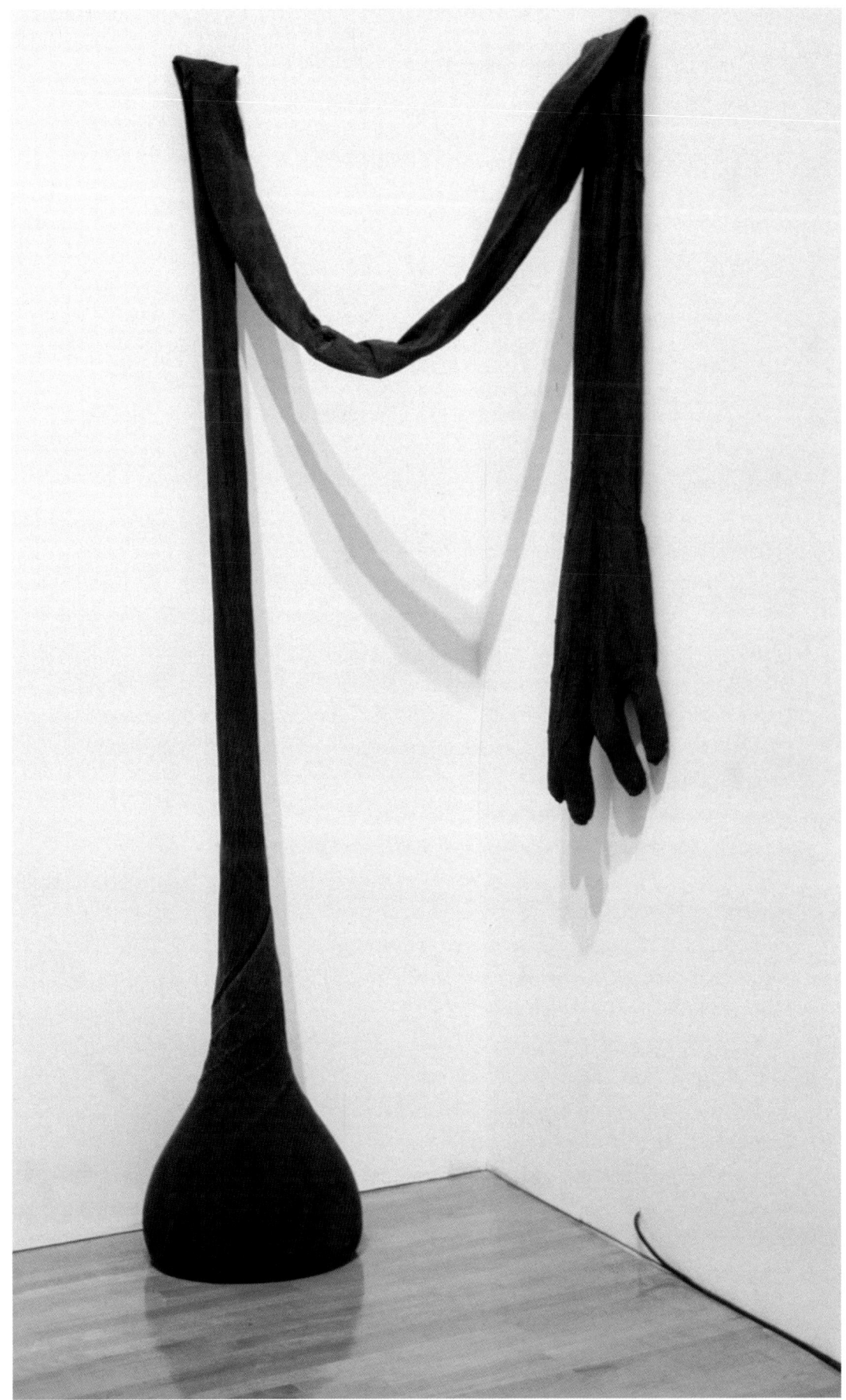

and cotton hangs from a hook in the ceiling; the extremities hang thigh-high with the ballast of twenty litres of water. They are sexy and irreverent "balls," obviously mimicking male genitalia. The sexually charged and suspended bulbous "containers" flip flop between stasis and dynamism, prompting onlookers to touch their taut surface/skin to animate some unknown potential. Should these *Strange Fruit* rise and fall depending on ascribed emotional states/social conditioning or wobble to and fro? There is an overriding urge to fondle them, guess their weight, suggest their incorporation in a sordid dramatic narrative without beginning or end — their potential seems lodged in a life-cycle narrative without closure.

The theatrical quality surrounding the motionless and anatomically incomplete (read: abstract) *Strange Fruit* is reminiscent of the dramatic artmaking strategies employed by abstract expressionist painting and John Cage's silences, "pregnant with unheard sounds."[3] The absence of the figure accentuates the high dramatic expectations of American painters like Johns and Rauschenberg and the minimal soundscapes of Cage, and likewise the spectacle in Dickson's *Strange Fruit*. It is "the body, both synecdochally in its parts and metonymically through its libidinal energies (that) was writ large in the abstract expressionist canvas... the phallus shut away (in its little 'closet'), the unmade bed emptied of the body(ies) that ravished its sheets."[4] The body may be shifting historically but expectations for a shared intuitive "presence" are no less loaded — and traces of this presence can be found in the hidden, fecund water of *Strange Fruit*. The onlooker may never see the growing slime and mold inside *Strange Fruit,* but the imagination traces this biological process to the bacterial composition of the absent body.

The active indifference of Dickson's spectacle is pervasive and tricky, resting as it does in the juxtaposition of transformal materials. Simple materials such as water, plaster, or hair are transformed into an integral, dynamic complex that is provocative or spectacular. For example, the fifty or more *Hair Drawings*, completed between 1990 and 1994 are composed of bonded layers of short hair from various sources, human pubis to horse. Dickson has created a spectrum of shapes, from a crown of thorns to swirling orbs, that are combined in wall-mounted installations to suggest an ephemeral cosmology without dominant shapes, apparent borders, or direction. The drawings are simply pinned to a wall, their flat, two-dimensional effect inviting closer inspection and assurances of familiarity. Viewing them is akin to surveying graffiti: the message approaches irrelevance when the aesthetic qualities of form are so strongly seductive and communicative. As individual drawings, very few of the *Hair Drawings* stand up to critical scrutiny but when collectively posted from floor to ceiling, the hair becomes a transforming agent: the *pressing* and *grouping* of the hair amplifies its ephemerality and its dramatic/comic resonance.

Opposite: John Dickson, *Rise and Fall* (1993)

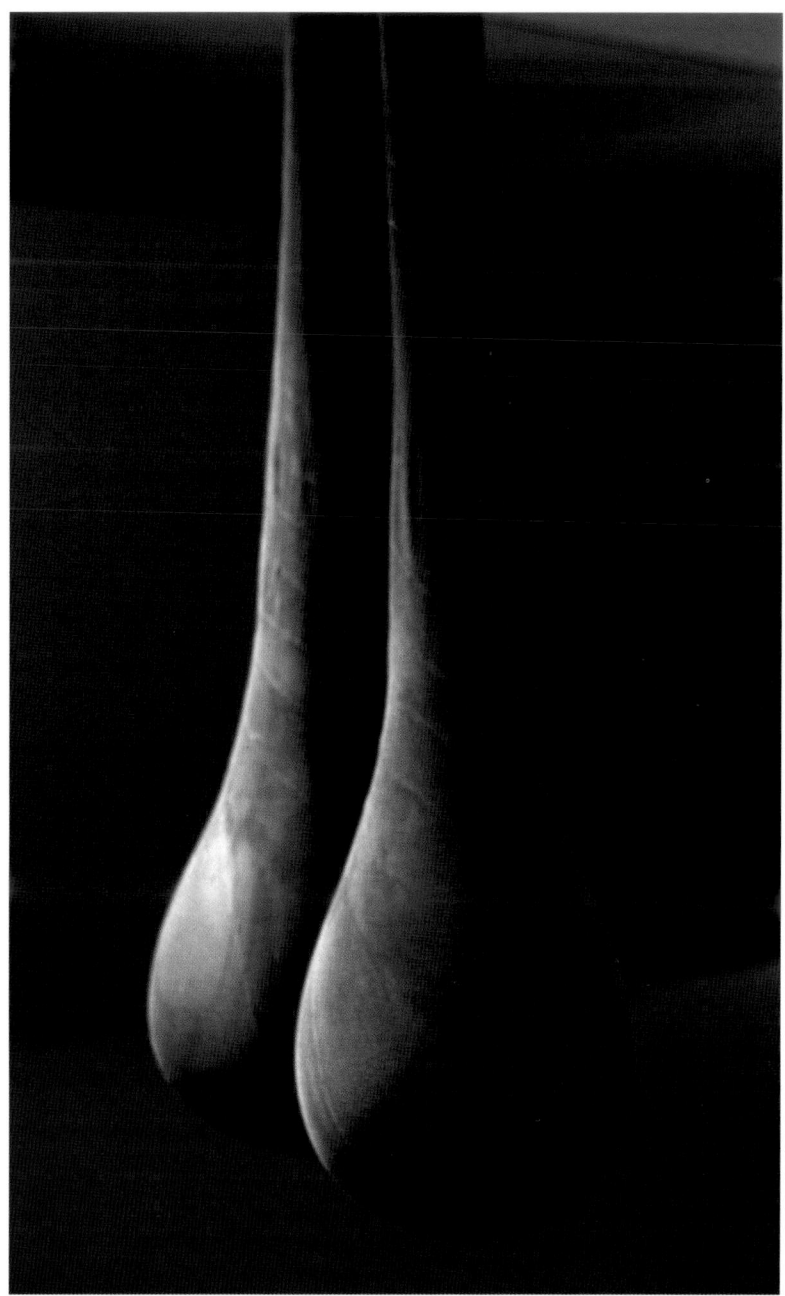

John Dickson, *Strange Fruit* (1993)

Water also becomes a powerful transforming agent in an important work from 1994, *Crying Eye*, a piece that elicits a cathartic response from onlookers while epitomizing the state of active indifference. So little happens, yet so many allusions are brought to life. A prosthetic eyeball and stylized socket are plastered into the surface of a white wall, disturbing the White Cube while producing a magnetic effect through its familiarity and the rush of contextual possibilities, both personal and social. If the viewer continues to inspect this detailed model of light and flesh, its low technology produces startling effects akin to filmic experience. The lower eye lid suddenly releases a tear which streams down the gallery wall, followed every seventeen seconds by another, and yet another, in an unending stream of tears. The eyeball stares out into the gallery void beyond the viewer, indifferent, constant and uncannily human in its ability to navigate between the poetic and the rational, between knowing and unknowing.

Sometimes this quality of active indifference is poignantly reserved and produces a beguiling sensation. Another piece, called *Rise and Fall* (1993), composed of an elongated rubberized sheath, a pump and timer, and water, acquires its expressiveness in the slight expanding and contracting of the work's upper section. A stylized hand forms the top section of the sheath and hangs downward, its performance deliberately constrained by the amount of oxygen supplied by a hidden pump. The hand quivers slightly and fails to erect itself; its pathetic gesture is life-affirming and yet also emulates the twitches of the body in death. The sculpture is plastic and dynamic, framed by a collage of the visual arts of sculpture, architecture, lighting and the rhythm and tempo of some dumb, perverse live performance.

Dickson's contrasting and complementary mission in the *Hair Drawings, Crying Eye* and *Rise and Fall* drive him systematically from the conceptual-art base he has inherited into a disquieting corner where Allan Sekula's "instrumental potential" comes to mind to engage "a silence that silences." Powerful, inexplicable images are produced when a kinetic or fluid element is introduced — barely breathing air, *Rise and Fall* speaks of struggle and of a collapse of time and space, a solace both fragmentary and ephemeral that fuses metaphor and literal reality as an important clue to unravelling a postmodern condition/psychology. This condition is largely an *expectant state* for the spectacle's development. *Rise and Fall's* anti-climactic flutter so constricts movement in space that without careful attention it appears to present a suspended phase of an unknown sequence. Performative movement, the active, disquieting element in spectacle is called into question. The cinematographic quality of movement, translated here into sculptural terms by dramatic lighting, sensuous forms and audio effects, presents an expressive quality that approaches the impact of edited film.

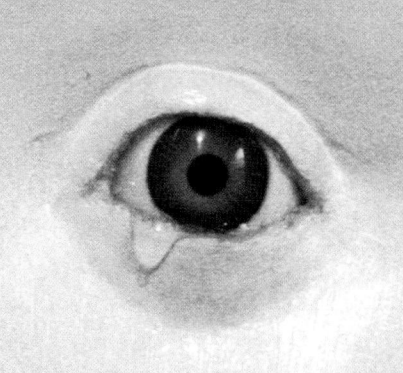

In *Vertigo*, the movement of water, light and the viewer's perspective create the illusion that the very same qualities of movement are suspended. In a darkened room, a blinking vortex of tiny white light bulbs suspended above an oval pool of water on the floor lulls the eyes and senses. The rhythmic counter-clockwise swirl of lights is a holding pattern for the eyes that generates a mesmerizing effect as it hovers above the unending whirlpool that "disappears" down a centripetal drain. If the onlooker gazes across the pool into the blinking vortex, s/he visually aligns a reflection of the sparkling vortex with the clockwise motion of the water as it enters its cycle around the drain. The illusion of a stationary ring of light is detected in the centre of the gleaming surface of the pool; all the while, an unending stereo-audio track of Dickson's voice counting backwards from 100 oscillates among the room's six speakers. Surface and content intersect so that a significant and fragile juncture is reached: "as the union of content and surface, the cross-section more than anything else conveys finality."[5]

Although the experiential, material and metaphorical qualities of the sculpture are developed as low technology, a significant point can be made about the spectacle that suspends underlying aspects of the creative process:

> The science of the engineer resembles that of the photographer; even when the photograph is to a large extent manipulated, as it was by the surrealists; it records what **is**, independently of how it is experienced.[6]

The intentional casualness of the works in the show underline the power of Dickson's low technology approach to producing minor spectacles, or what might be called *newly configured spectacles* that are part absurdity, part transformational in nature. Dickson's sculptures combine and juxtapose simple, low-cost materials and movement to establish a sensibility that inadvertently recodes and challenges our understanding of the spectacular as that which dazzles and produces a consensual break or rupture with tradition. *Vertigo*, like the other sculptures in the exhibition, does much to promote a reconciliation with sculpture's lost but grand potential (in public sculpture) by capitalizing on sculpture's inability to transfer any shared meaning and values, substituting instead a rare and powerful sense of wonder and accomplishment.

Opposite: John Dickson, *Crying Eye* (1994)

Endnotes

1. Louis Begley, "Time is Everything," *New Yorker* (October 16, 1995): 156.

2. A lengthy footnote of introduction to Dickson's issues and strategies is attributed to the artist himself (1996). It may well be the most illuminating source of information about Dickson's work. He says, "I have continued working with water because I find it under-explored in terms of its sculptural and conceptual possibilities. The strong psychological and physiological effect water can have on us, its physical versatility, and the richness of its symbolism make it a deeply satisfying substance to work with. By concentrating on water as a consistent medium I am narrowing my field of vision enough to focus my concerns without limiting the range of possibilities.

    "When I first began working with water, it represented a generalized bodily fluid, lewd and animalistic in its references to piss, come, milk and saliva (*Garden of Delights*). In the following series, *Strange Fruit*, the water spoke of a fleshy fecundity, suggested by the pressure of water against rubberized canvas. In the recent installation pieces, direct references to the body have been replaced by the viewer's own body. The character of the water has become broader, embodying a wide range of ideas, all at odds with the rectilinear, the fixed, and the finite. In these pieces, water has come to represent a generalized natural force that is contrary to logic and to the rigid order that we attempt to impose upon the world. I associate this force with intuition, emotion, the organic, to fertility, growth, vitality. Yet it is also aligned with destruction, death and chaos, because it is intimately connected to change and unpredictability. The recent installation piece, *Vertigo*, places the viewer in situations which attempt to upset their notions of order and control, by challenging their assumptions about what is fixed and constant.

    "In *Vertigo* I have used the spiralling form of a whirling galaxy, a black whirlpool, and a revolving sound element to physically and perceptually create a sense of rotation that has a mesmerizing, hypnotic affect. Hundreds of white, chasing Christmas lights illusionistically create a a spinning galaxy, that turns inwards towards its center. The galaxy is reflected in a double thickness of glass so that it appears to be floating beyond the confines of the room. It is mimicked by the slow turning of the dark vortex of water. A recorded voice counting backwards from 100 to negative 100, moves around the space, by means of an arrangement of six speakers, situating the viewer inside a revolving system... The viewer is placed in a situation which has a strong psychological affect but rather than anxiety, one is lulled into semi-consciousness, resembling the state just before sleep."

3. See Caroline A. Jones, "Finishing School: John Cage and the Abstract Expressionist Ego," *Critical Inquiry* 19 (Summer 1993, No. 4): 653.

4. Ibid.

5. Ben van Berkel & Caroline Bos, *Delinquent Visionaries* (Rotterdam: 010 Publishers, 1993), 62.

6. Allan Sekula, "The Body and the Archive," *The Contest of Meaning: Critical Histories of Photography*, ed. Richard Bolton (London: MIT Press, 1992), 344.

Opposite: John Dickson, *Vertigo* (1995)

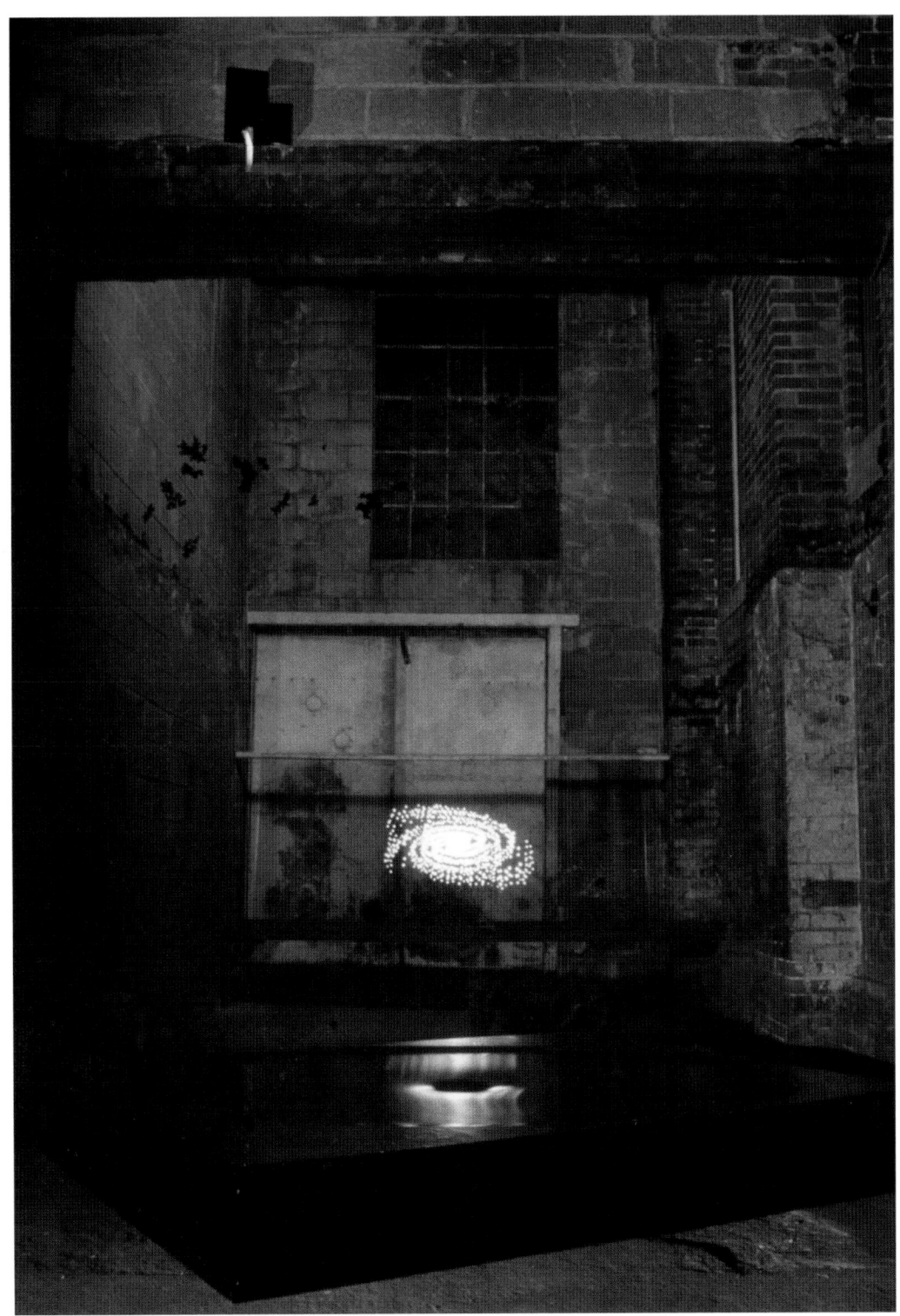

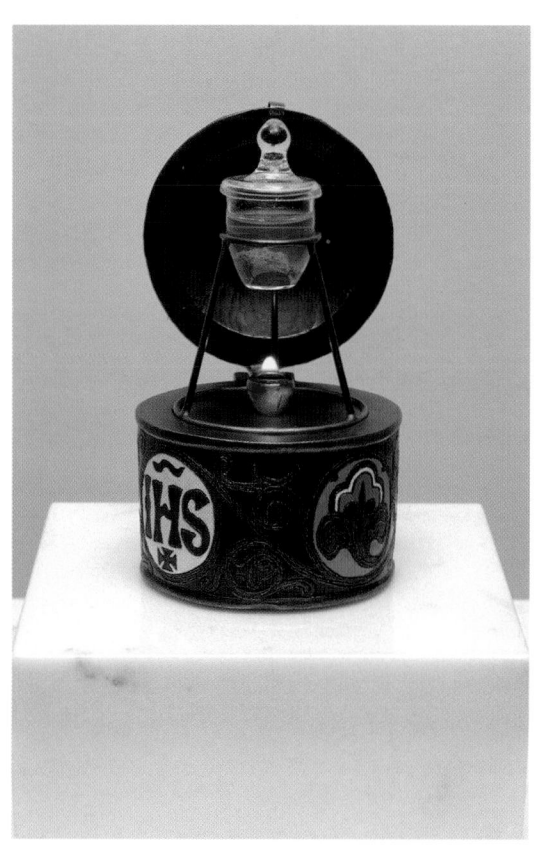

Laurie Walker, *Pyx* (1995) (Detail)

Laurie Walker:

RESURRECTED

Nancy Campbell

Let us start with the Last Supper. Piero Camporesi writes in his essay *The Consecrated Host: A Wondrous Excess* that the:

> awesomeness of the sacrifice (being that of Christ in the Roman Catholic tradition) caused the dislocation of natural laws. It violated them through a series of impossible alchemic reactions that upset the relationship between substances and their accidents. Color, odor, flavor survived the annihilation of the substances that expressed them. By turning into flesh and blood, the primary substances — bread and wine — changed radically in essence, but their physical attributes survived their metamorphosis. The sacrifice turned the inanimate into the animate. The life of the heavenly enzyme, the Incorruptible, fermented out of unleavened bread. Vital, vivifying, beautifying food was born out of dead food.[1]

Transubstantiation is the assimilation of the divine into the human which permits the fusion of the human with the divine. This cycle involves a transcendent belief that the object has value greater than its inanimate self, that it can signify, essentially, new life.

This is a rather ominous departure point for the consideration of art. The idea of transubstantiation implies that objects such as bread and wine are not metaphors for the body but the body itself. Transformation is a more often used term when discussing the connection of the arts to the real world. It is standard practice for an artist to "transform" an object, make it *seem* to be something other than what it actually is through the manipulation of materials and metaphor.

Transmutation is another term that implies changing states. Historically the term transmutation is rooted in alchemy — a traditional chemical philosophy involving the changing of base material into gold — allowing for materials to assume a higher form. The alchemist held seemingly magical powers by which he effected the process of transmuting. I would compare an artist to an alchemist; however, it is the viewer's interpretation of the magic that is the transmutation.

This preliminary discussion of terminology is more than an exercise in semantics. These three principles of change — transubstantiation, transformation, and transmutation — are particularly useful to recall when reflecting on the work of Montreal artist Laurie Walker. She uses transubstantiation and transmutation as a source of metaphor or symbol to bring about transformation. She offers a wide range of objects and materials, each loaded with metaphor and pristinely crafted, presented in clever juxtaposition. It is the delight of piecing ideas and references together that gives strength to the work. Many of Walker's references are based in western mythology and religion. It is not her intent to use these sources as critique, but rather as vehicles for the consideration of transubstantiation and transmutation. This labyrinth of ideas and materials allows each viewer to access Walker's art personally in order to reflect on the cyclical nature of life and the spirit.

In *Pyx* (1995) one can connect the notion of transubstantiation to the Host. A pyx is an ornamental vessel or casket, usually constructed out of precious metal, in which the Host is kept. Through an understanding of transubstantiation and the purpose of the pyx we can compare the delicate object, constructed by the artist herself, to a coffin or casket literally intended to hold the Divine flesh. The enamel pyx is marked with the letters IHS, which is a standard inscription on many pyx. These letters, adopted from the Latin *in hoc signo, in hac salus*, or *Iesous Hominum Salvator*, refer to Jesus Christ. Walker's version of the tiny vessel replaces the Host with a flame, above which sits a tiny crucible. Historically, the crucible was used by alchemists to melt metals or minerals. Here, the crucible heats a tiny wad of clay. Clay could be read here as a metaphor for the creation of human beings as seen in Genesis II.7 — or in terms of artmaking. In the context in which Walker places the clay it also refers to the transubstantiated body or an alchemic experiment.

Hive (1996) replicates a traditionally shaped beehive which would have been constructed out of straw. Walker's is made of wax; however, instead of the product of bees she uses paraffin, a by-product of oil refineries produced by humans. Trapped within the structure are hundreds of dead bees, seemingly victims of their environment. It is said that of all insects bees are the closest to man. Shakespeare echoes this sociological view in *Henry V*:

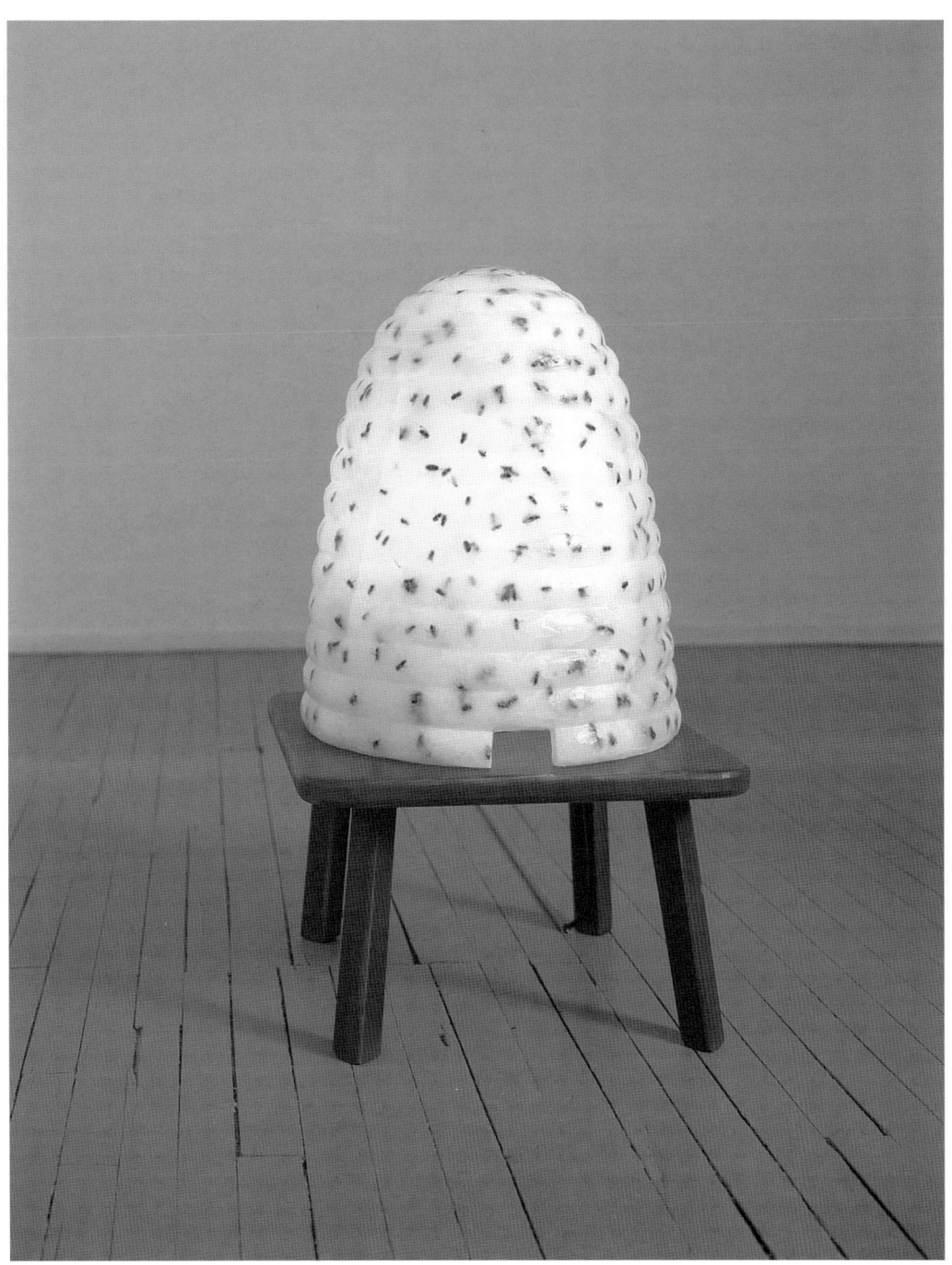

Laurie Walker, *Hive* (1996)

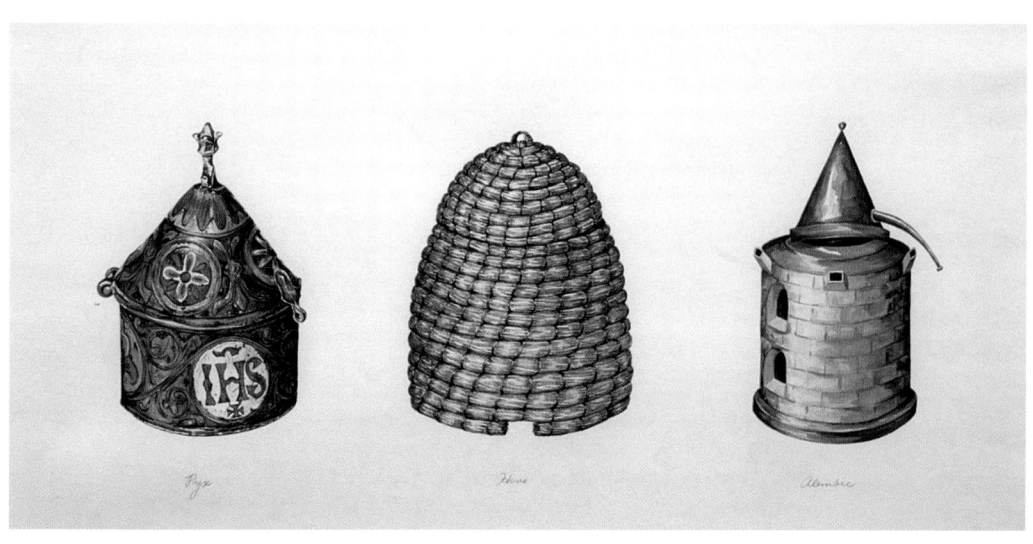

Laurie Walker, *Pyx, Hive, Alembic* (1996)

> for so work the honey-bees
> Creatures that, by a rule of nature, teach
> The art of order to a peopled kingdom.[2]

The fact remains that people do not know what causes the collective will of the hive, what causes total integration and co-operation in building the comb, care for the larvae, or mutual feeding. This intricate system, like the systems of religion, holds no answers or no known scientific rationale, though it fascinates and provides participants with promise of a better life. We can view the hive, like the pyx, as a vessel for a system.

Transubstantiation is also interesting to consider here.

> Just as honey lends its own incorruptibility to the fruit that is dipped in it,
> so does the body of the Savior, in joining ours, lend us some of the seeds
> of immortality He served, and the special right to live forever.[3]

Like the Host, honey is seen to hold magical regenerative powers. Honey is the by-product of a successful, vital hive. Nature (or more specifically pollen) is transmuted into honey and harvested from the hive. Similarly the Host becomes the transubstantiated body held within the pyx. The pyx and the hive are brought together by Walker in a beautiful watercolour rendering titled *Pyx, Hive, Alembic* (1996). The pyx and the hive are united with an alembic — an alembic being a container that tests, purifies or transforms, and historically a chamber or vessel used for distilling. The alembic further informs the connection between the pyx and the hive.

Prayer Beads again recalls transubstantiation through its materials — flesh and wine. Walker covered a number of small loaf-size rocks with pigs' bladders. Each bladder was carefully stitched around a drilled rock and over time it has dried and formed a strong but crusty skin. The rocks are linked together by a clear plastic tube forming the exaggerated shape of traditional prayer beads, or a rosary, on the floor. The tube is filled with wine which flows through the fleshy rocks, enlivening the inanimate forms. Reference is made to the transformative powers of religion and the transcendent belief in everlasting life — as Giacomo Correglia put it in his *Practica del confessionario* "salubrious elixir vitae of His blood." The rocks, however, maintain a connection to the earth.

Seeing Blue (1993–94) although not intended as a partner piece to *Prayer Beads* offers many similarities. The main component of the work is a large sponge, approximately the size of a garden shed, which is meticulously carved to resemble a human brain. From this central piece circulate tubes, a wire armature, burettes, all the essential scientific equipment standardly used in experiments. Within this system of tube and wire flows a blue liquid, the lifeblood of this mutant brain. The liquid appears to flow from the brain through tubing into

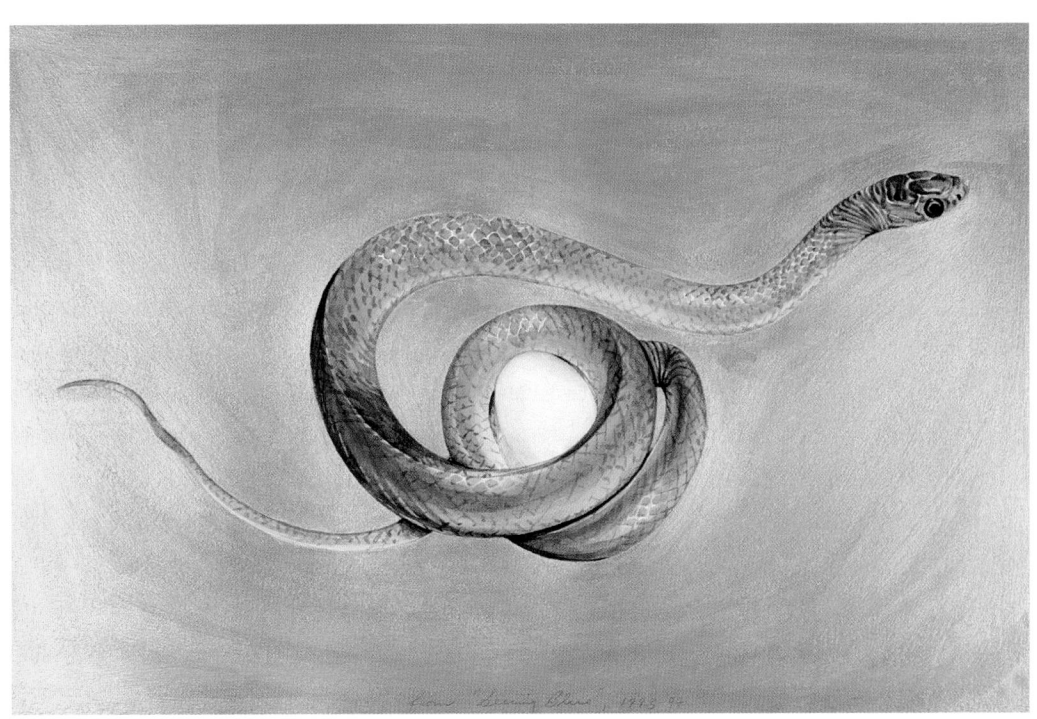

Laurie Walker, *From "Seeing Blue", 1993–94*

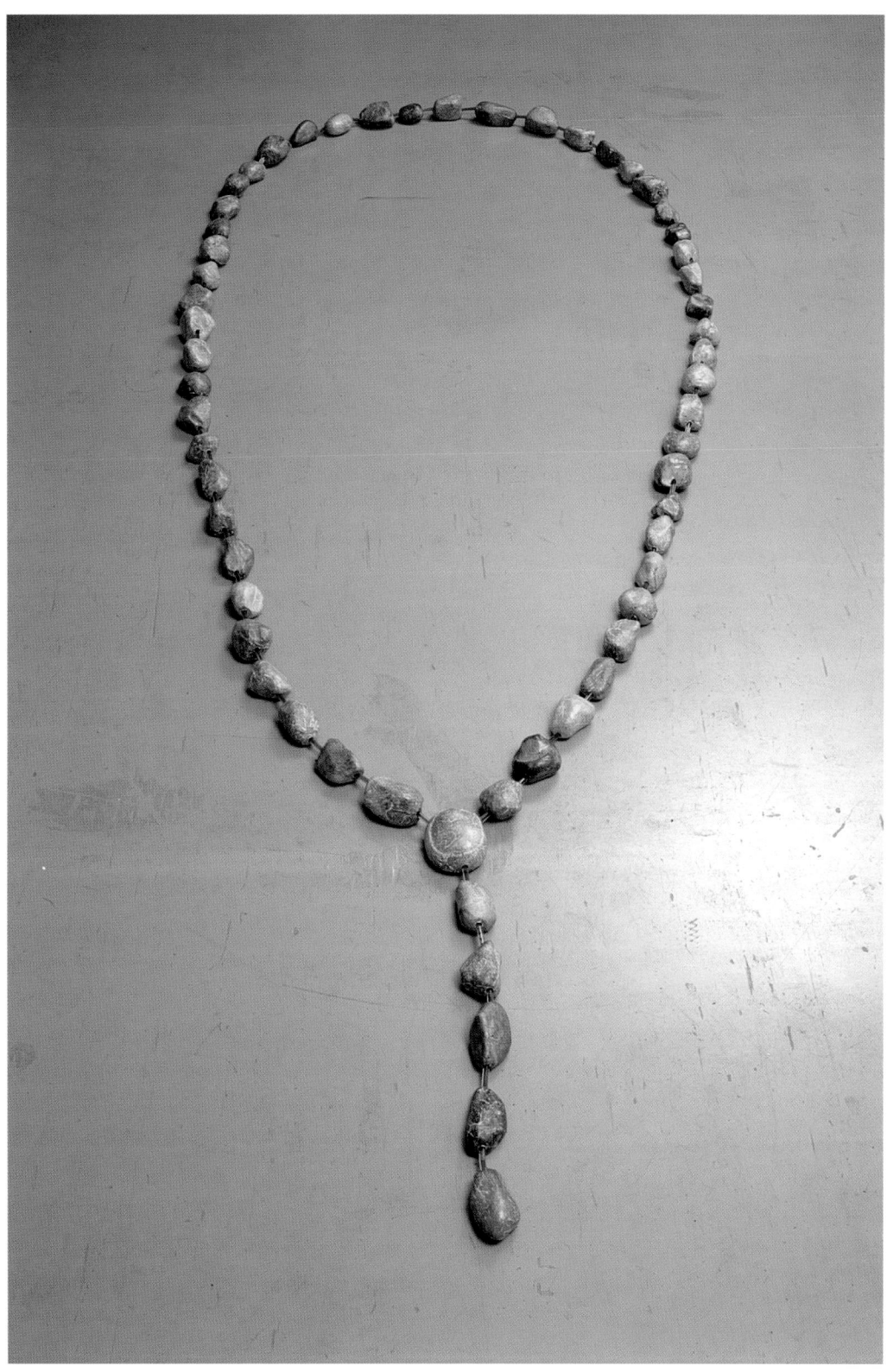

Laurie Walker, *Prayer Beads* (1995)

two burettes. A burette is a glass tube with a stop cork at the bottom which regulates the flow of liquid through its chambers. It is also interesting to note here that historically the word *burette* comes from the Old French word *cruet* meaning "a vessel for sacrificial wine." In this work, the burettes regulate the flow of the blue liquid into two hollow eggshells, which when filled with the dark liquid resemble eyeballs. From the eggs the liquid flows through a tube encircling the brain. The liquid then re-enters the brain, resulting in an area of greenish saturation. One reading of the piece allows for the consideration of transmutation. The blue liquid leaves the brain (body) and through some sort of mutation within the eggs re-enters the brain as food or sustenance. Like the wine, the blue liquid becomes blood recalling the life cycle. *Seeing Blue* is appended with six exquisitely rendered watercolours to affirm this reading. Rebirth and creation are represented in the symbols Walker uses in these works. The egg, for example, is representative of birth. The ouroborous (a snake swallowing its own tail) represents the life cycle of evolution.

Ashen Wing (1995) a bird's wing covered on the top side by ashes derived from wood and palm leaves, and the underside appliquéd with a mirrored surface, refers to resurrection. The wing refers to the story of the phoenix. Depending on your source, the phoenix lives up to 500 or 600 years before it burns itself on a pyre and dies in order to rise from the ashes young and beautiful to live another cycle. By immolating itself over and over again the phoenix has become a symbol for immortality. Like the wine and the Host, the phoenix offers the possibility of eternal life. The mirrored surface on the underside of the wing puts the viewers in the position of seeing themselves and becoming players in the eternal life cycle of which the artist speaks.

Like alchemic reactions, the work of Laurie Walker intends to upset the relationship between substances and their accidents. Like the wine and the Host, her objects change radically in essence but their physical attributes survive their metamorphosis. Her objects, whether a pyx or hive, rocks or a brain, reanimate or resurrect themselves within the context in which they are presented. Essentially, through Walker's meticulous and engaging practice we are allowed a glimpse of the transformative power of artmaking; we witness the possibility of vital, vivifying, beautifying food born out of dead food.

Endnotes

1. Piero Camporesi, "The Consecrated Host: A Wondrous Excess," *Zone 3: Fragments for a History of the Human Body, Part One,* ed. Michael Feher with Ramona Naddaff and Nadia Tazi (New York: Zone Books, 1989), 226.

2. *Henry V*, act 1. scene 2.

3. Piero Camporesi, "The Consecrated Host: A Wondrous Excess," *Zone 3: Fragments for a History of the Human Body, Part One,* ed. Michael Feher with Ramona Naddaff and Nadia Tazi (New York: Zone Books, 1989), 227.

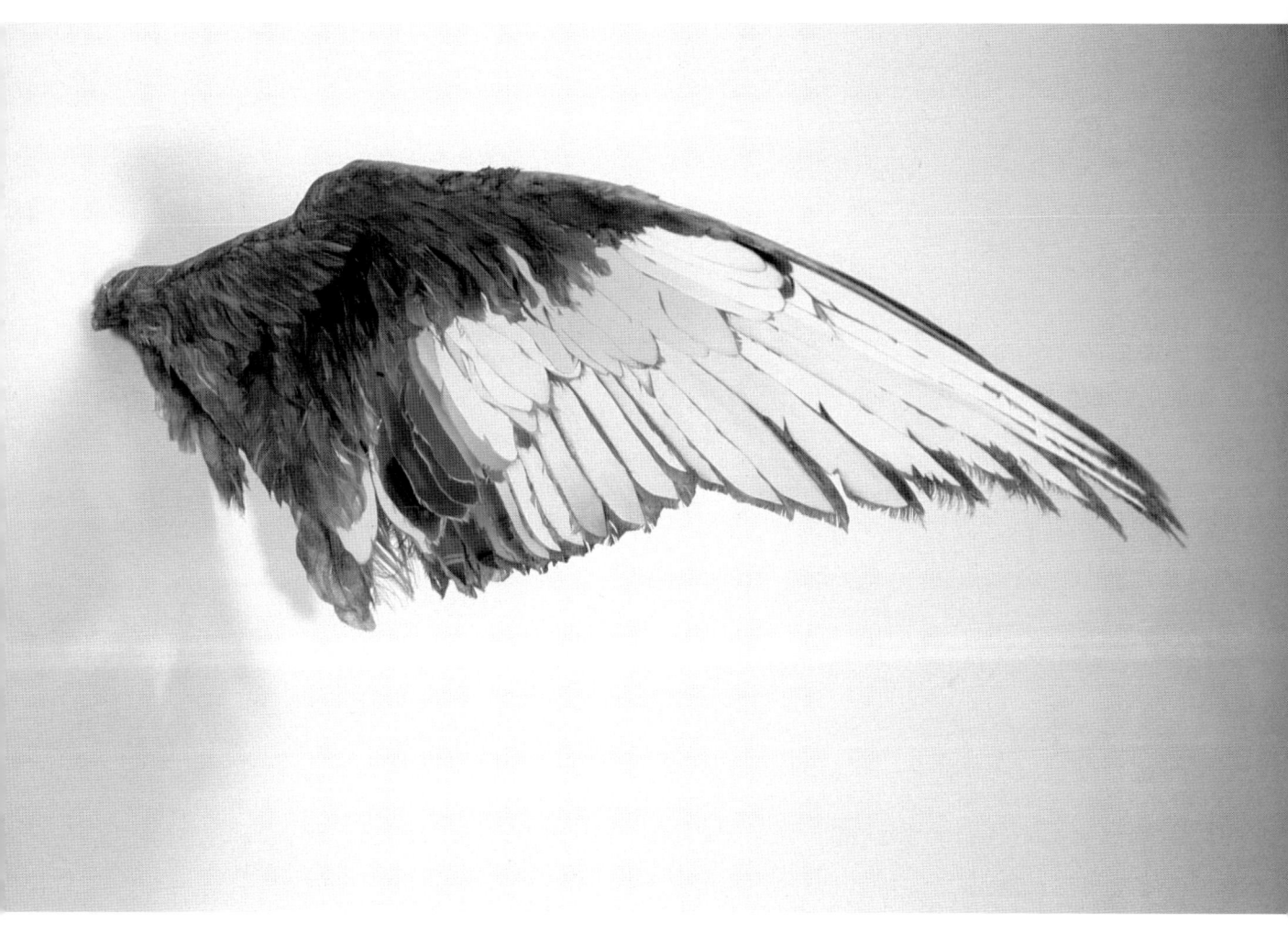

Laurie Walker, *Ashen Wing* (1995)

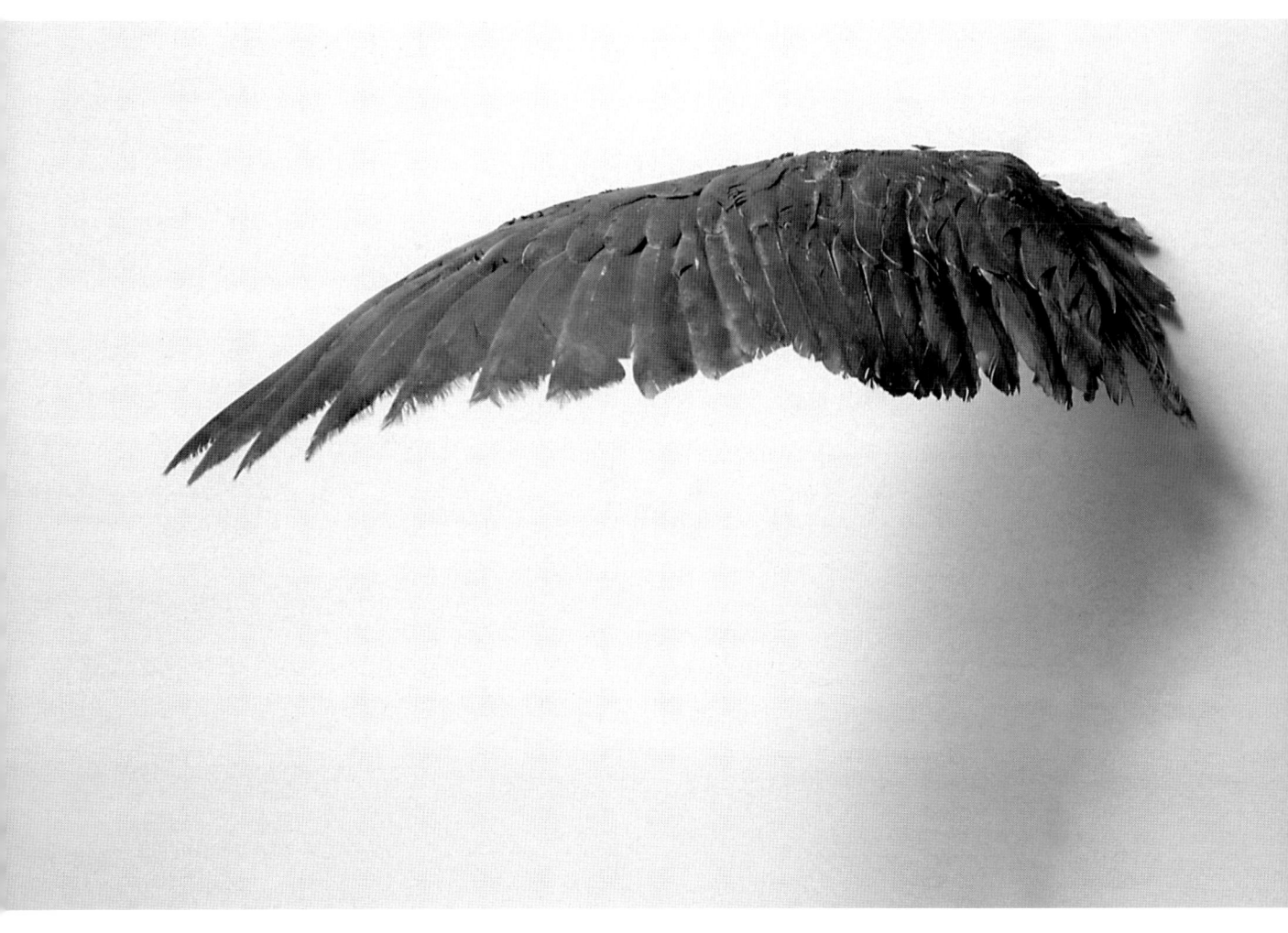

Laurie Walker, *Ashen Wing* (1995)

LIST OF CONTRIBUTORS

—◆—

Jan Allen is Curator of Contemporary Art at the Agnes Etherington Art Centre. Recent exhibitions include *The Female Imaginary* (1994), *Rx: Taking Our Medicine* (1995), and *Fertile Ground* (1996).

Wayne Baerwaldt has been involved with Plug In Inc., for eight years as director, fundraiser and curator. He is currently an adjunct curator with Plug In and the development officer for Archive Conz, Verona. He has organized exhibitions such as *Endart* at Ace Art (1988), *Under the Influence of Fluxus* (1991), the *Multi-Culti-Queer Pavilion* (1992), *Pierre Molinier* (1993), *Dark O'Clock* (1995) and *Juan Davila — Winnipeg Strike 1919–1995*.

Nancy Campbell has been curator at the Macdonald Stewart Art Centre since 1991. Her projects include international group exhibitions *Frankenstein: Explorations in Manipulation and Surrationality* (1994) and *Living Units* (1996). Survey exhibitions include work with artists Stan Douglas, Christine Davis, Kim Adams, and Robert Flack. Campbell serves on the Board at the Toronto Sculpture Garden.

JOHN DICKSON

——◆——

Born in 1961, London, England

Lives and works in Toronto

EDUCATION

1989   Master of Fine Arts — Sculpture, York
        University, North York

1986   Bachelor of Fine Arts, Queen's University,
        Kingston

SELECTED EXHIBITIONS

1996   *Container 96*
        Copenhagen, Denmark.

        Rise and Fall
        Plug In Inc., Winnipeg, Manitoba
        Agnes Etherington Art Centre, Kingston
        Macdonald Stewart Art Centre, Guelph

1995   *Nether Mind*
        Toronto

        Hermit IV — The Meridian Crossings
        The Plasy Monastery, Czech Republic

1994   *Hydrophobia*
        Project Room, Galerie Optica: Montreal

        Duke-u-menta
        Duke of Connaught Hotel, Toronto

        Naked State: A Selected View of Toronto Art
        The Power Plant, Toronto

        Halo
        Garnet Press Gallery, Toronto

1993   *Manual*
        Garnet Press, Toronto

        Nether Mind
        Toronto

        John Dickson, Greg Hefford, Lyla Rye
        The Koffler Loggia Gallery, North York

        Hair Drawings
        Extension Gallery, The Print and Drawing
        Council of Canada, Toronto

1992   *Nether Mind*
        Toronto

1991   *Nether Mind*
        Toronto

1989   *Consumed*
        White Water Gallery, North Bay

EXHIBITION CATALOGUES

Dewdney, Christopher. *Nether Mind*. Toronto:
Nether Mind, 1995.

Dompierre, Louise. *Naked State: A Selected View of
Toronto Art*. Toronto: The Power Plant, 1994.

Holubizky, Ihor. *Nether Mind*. Toronto: Nether Mind,
1993.

SELECTED BIBLIOGRAPHY

Collins, Curtis J. "John Dickson, Galerie Optica."
Parachute 78 (May 1995): 53–54.

Dault, Gary Michael. "Young Toronto." *Canadian Art*
11 (Winter 1994): 57–67.

Hanna, Deirdre. "Dickson's Fountain Halo." *Now
Magazine* (Toronto), June 16–22, 1994.

Lehmann, Henry. "Optica Vision." *The Mirror* 10
(Dec.8–15, 1994): 43.

LAURIE WALKER

—◆—

Born in 1962, Montreal, Quebec

Lives and works in Montreal

EDUCATION

1987   Masters of Fine Arts, Nova Scotia College of
        Art and Design, Halifax

1984   Bachelor of Fine Arts, Mount Allison
        University, Sackville

SELECTED EXHIBITIONS

1996   *Rise and Fall*
        Agnes Etherington Art Centre, Kingston
        Macdonald Stewart Art Centre, Guelph

        Galerie Christiane Chassay, Montreal

1994   *Laurie Walker — Seeing Blue*
        Musée d'art contemporain de Montréal

        Laurie Walker — A Material Writing of Things
        Oakville Galleries, Oakville

1993   Galerie Christiane Chassay, Montreal

1991   Galerie Christiane Chassay, Montreal

1990   *Laurie Walker*
        Southern Alberta Art Gallery, Lethbridge

1989   *Eye of Nature*
        Walter Phillips Gallery, Banff

        Galerie Christiane Chassay, Montreal

SELECTED EXHIBITION CATALOGUES

Augaitis, Daina, Helga Pakasaar, eds. *Eye of Nature*.
Banff: Walter Phillips Gallery, 1991.

Fischer, Barbara. *Laurie Walker — A Material Writing of
Things*. Oakville: Oakville Galleries, 1994.

Landry, Pierre. *Laurie Walker — Seeing Blue*. Montreal:
Musée d'art contemporain de Montréal, 1994.

SELECTED BIBLIOGRAPHY

Armstrong, John. "Laurie Walker." *C Magazine* 43
(Autumn 1994): 65.

Grande, John K. "Laurie Walker." *Artforum* 31
(Summer 1993): 116.

Johnstone, Lesley. "Oscillations." *Vanguard* 17
(April/May 1988): 40.

Lachance, Michael. "Transfusion bleue," *Spirale* 134
(Summer 1994): 24.

Rondos, Spyro. "Laurie Walker." *Parachute* 76
(Autumn 1994): 57–58.

Taillefer, Hélène. "Vertiges Métaphoriques," *Espace* 17
(Autumn 1991): 42–43.

LIST OF WORKS

———◆———

John Dickson

Hair Drawings (1990-94)
   human and animal hair fixed with acrylic spray and
   pinned directly to the wall
   installation size variable

Tornado (1994)
   human hair fixed with acrylic spray and pinned directly
   to the wall
   84 x 50 cm

Strange Fruit (1993)
   canvas, rubber latex, water, steel hook
   71 x 25 x 76 cm

Rise and Fall (1993)
   water, rubberized canvas, pump, electronic timer
   hand – 46 x 25 x 76 cm

Crying Eye (1994)
   life-size plastic eye inset into drywall, I.V. tap, water

Vertigo (1995)
   chasing Christmas lights reflected in glass, whirlpool,
   pump, audio system with six speakers
   whirlpool – 240 x 195 x 30 cm

All works courtesy of the Artist.

Laurie Walker

Seeing Blue (1993–94)
   installation with six watercolours
   sculpture: synthetic sponge, egg shells, plastic tubing,
   coloured liquid, burettes, bronze, stainless steel, clamps,
   painted steel
   399 x 335 cm diameter

   works on paper:
   From "Seeing Blue", 1993–94
   watercolour on Arches paper
   52.2 x 74.2 cm
   Spill, from "Seeing Blue", 1993–94
   watercolour and pencil crayon on Arches paper
   71 x 54 cm
   Three Flowers of Alchemy, from "Seeing Blue", 1993–94
   watercolour and acrylic on Arches paper
   50.9 x 35.1 cm
   Ouroboros, from "Seeing Blue", 1993–94
   watercolour on Arches paper
   39.1 x 44.8 cm
   From "Seeing Blue", 1993–94
   watercolour and acrylic on Arches paper
   31.4 x 46.9 cm
   "I thirst", from "Seeing Blue", 1993–94
   watercolour on Arches paper
   68.5 x 48.5 cm

Prayer Beads (1995)
   rocks, pigs' bladders, thread, plastic tubing, red wine
   9 x 155 x 412 cm

Ashen Wing (1995)
   bird's wing, ashes of palm leaves and wood, mirrorized
   plastic
   17 x 25 x 65 cm

Pyx (1995)
   enamelled and patinated bronze, pyrex crucible, clay in
   liquid, wick, lamp oil, flame
   14 x 8.5 x 18 cm

Hive (1996)
   paraffin wax, dead bees, rotating light, painted wood
   77 x 45 x 45 cm

Pyx, Hive, Alembic (1996)
   watercolour on Arches paper
   37.5 x 72 cm

All works courtesy of the Artist and Galerie Christiane
Chassay, Montreal with the exception of *Seeing Blue*
(1993–94), courtesy of Musée d'art contemporain de
Montréal.

ACKNOWLEDGEMENTS

◆

The catalogue *Rise and Fall: John Dickson and Laurie Walker* is co-published by Plug In Inc., the Agnes Etherington Art Centre, and the Macdonald Stewart Art Centre in conjunction with exhibitions held at Plug In Inc. March 15 to April 10, 1996, the Agnes Etherington Art Centre July 7 to September 8, 1996 and at the Macdonald Stewart Art Centre November 21 to January 26, 1997.

Support of The Canada Council is acknowledged for assistance towards the exhibition presentation and publication.

The exhibition *John Dickson: Rise and Fall* at Plug In Inc. received support from the Manitoba Arts Council, the City of Winnipeg, St. Norbert Arts and Cultural Centre, WH & SE Loewen Foundation, Jon Tupper, Pedro Mendes, Jean LeMaitre, Noam Gonick, Laura Michalchyshyn, Stephen Andrews, Micah Lexier, Sheila Spence, Alison Norlen, Sig Laser, Neil Minuk, Scott Barnham, Cliff Eyland, John Maclean, Christine Kirouac, Jon Jonasson.

The exhibitions and programmes at the Agnes Etherington Art Centre receive financial support from the Ontario Arts Council, Queen's University, the City of Kingston, and the Townships of Kingston and Pittsburgh.

The Macdonald Stewart Art Centre is supported by the City of Guelph, County of Wellington, Wellington Board of Education and the University of Guelph, and the Ontario Government through the Ministry of Culture, Tourism and Recreation and the Ontario Arts Council.

Photography:
    John Dickson: pp. 7-9, 17, 18, 22, 24, 27; Denis Farley: pp. 12, 13, courtesy of Musée d'art contemporain de Montréal; Guy L'Heureux: p. 34; Paul Litherland: p. 28, 31, 32, 35, 37, 38.
Design:
    Julie Gibb & Christian Morrison, Greenstreet Design
Editing for Macdonald Stewart Art Centre:
    Anne McPherson
Copy Editing:
    Karen Mac Cormack
Scanning and Separations:
    Douglas Laxdal, The GAS Company
Printing:
    C.J. Graphics Inc., Toronto
Cover Images:
    Detail from John Dickson's *Vertigo* and detail from Laurie Walker's *Seeing Blue*.

ISBN 0-88911-706-3